Spiked Helmets of Imperial Germany

I
II
III
IV
V
VI
VII
VIII

I
II
III
IV
V
VI
VII
VIII

SPIKED HELMETS

of

IMPERIAL GERMANY

Cavalry
Artillery
Train

Tony Cowan & Wm. Randall Trawnik

Schiffer Military History
Atglen, PA

Book Design by Ian Robertson.

Library of Congress Control Number: 2005921418

Printed in China.
ISBN: 0-7643-2167-6

Published by Schiffer Publishing Ltd.
4880 Lower Valley Road
Atglen, PA 19310
Phone: (610) 593-1777
FAX: (610) 593-2002
E-mail: Info@schifferbooks.com.
Visit our web site at: www.schifferbooks.com
Please write for a free catalog.
This book may be purchased from the publisher.
Please include $3.95 postage.
Try your bookstore first.

In Europe, Schiffer books are distributed by:
Bushwood Books
6 Marksbury Avenue
Kew Gardens
Surrey TW9 4JF
England
Phone: 44 (0) 20 8392-8585
FAX: 44 (0) 20 8392-9876
E-mail: info@bushwoodbooks.co.uk.
Free postage in the UK. Europe: air mail at cost.
Try your bookstore first.

Contents

Foreword

The Pickelhauben, or spiked helmet, is the salient identifying military article of the Imperial German Nation. Perhaps more importantly, it was also an icon depicting an age of splendor and grandeur that will never be seen again. Today it is difficult to realize how these wonderful pieces played such an important role not only in Germany, but in many other countries as well. The spiked helmet may be considered the ultimate artifact in the history of military uniforms. It is our fervent hope that in some small way these books will help to preserve a portion of this grand era and allow the reader a glimpse of the magnificence of this time.

It has been a privilege, for myself and my good friend, Randy Trawnik, to have met so many wonderful people in our research travels. Our common interest and shared camaraderie have made us many new and good friends. Again, we would like to thank them and their families for their gracious hospitality.

The second book of the trilogy *Spiked Helmets of Imperial Germany* addresses all mounted military units of the Imperial Army, including Cavalry, Artillery, and Trains.

We leave for the third book all the pieces that we felt did not properly fit into the first two volumes. Some of the items to be included will be the Flugeladjutants, early pieces, wartime pieces, beamte, customs, and nonmilitary helmets. Also included will be a section on field covers and their development.

Foreword

It is our wish to dedicate this book in memory of our mothers, Rubie Wynalene Carter Cowan and Renate Mathilde Dorothea Trankner Trawnik, without whose unwavering faith and support in their sons we would be the lesser for.

We would like to thank our wives, Kathy Cowan and Marcie Trawnik, as well as our children, for their patience and understanding over the years with our avid pursuit of this arcane hobby.

It has been our great pleasure to share this interest with many good collector friends. It is their encouragement that helps fuel our enthusiasm for this subject and assures its ongoing tradition. It is with heartfelt gratitude that we thank the following people:

We extend a special thanks to Charles van Hoenacker, who has shared his knowledge, collection, and his beautiful home and family with us.

Remy Schcall, who has enthusiastically shared with us his collection, and joined us in our research travels.

Walt Hartman, as a traveling companion and his sharing of resources.

Harry Fakner, for sharing his collection, home, and family with us.

Brian Sanders, for sharing his collection with us.

John Sandidge, for allowing us to use some of his wonderful pieces.

To all our fine collector friends, without whose support and contributions this work would not have been possible.

Help keep the tradition alive.

To our readers

Ein voellig und einwandfreies Werk ueber Pickelhauben scheint niemanden zu gelingen. Noch sind immer Fehler zu berichtigen und Luecken zu fuellen. Vielen Dank fuer euer verstandnis.

A complete and absolutely correct study of spiked helmets is impossible to do. There will always be corrections to be made and holes to fill. Many thanks for your understanding.

Flag presentation.

Introduction:
Helmets of the Prussian Garde du Corps, Garde Kurassier and Kurassier, Saxon Garde Reiter, and Garde Karabinder

The leather-spiked helmet of 1842 preceded the introduction of the metal heavy cavalry helmet of the kurassier regiments by one year. The Garde du Corps and Garde Kurassier and Kurassier were first introduced in 1843. The kurassier helmet, nicknamed "lobster tail helmet" due to its long scalloped back visor was used initially by only Prussian heavy cavalry regiments. The style of helmet also influenced the helmets used by the Jaeger zu Pferde (Mounted Riflemen) units formed by Prussia in the early 1900's. The "kurassier" pattern was later adopted in 1876 by Saxony for its Garde Reiter and Karabinier heavy cavalry units.

The metal helmet adopted in 1843 was tall and massive. The front visor was hinged and hung on the outside of the body so it could actually be raised. All the bodies are metal, either tombac or steel, and all wore rounded scales. All rear visors were either made in separate segments or were constructed to have that appearance. This has given these helmets the nickname of "lobster-tails". The Officer helmet had a spike base, which is a stylized cross pediment. The throat of the spike base had vents on each side. These appeared as a Maltese cross formed by four cutouts with the cross at their center. The base was attached with domed screws. The spike was fluted and tapered. The fluted ridges extend out at the base of the spike and the space between them as an inward curve from one to the other formed a six-sided floriform effect. All officer helmets exhibited a ridge just behind the spike base. The chinscales were affixed with a stylized screw post passing through a three lobed retainer known as the cloverleaf rosettes or the German word, "kleeblatten". The cockade (kokarde) was large with serrated edges and a metal striated ring about two thirds of the way out from the center. Kokarden were painted with the state color and the national colors. The visors were lined with either a fine leather of velvet material. The helmet used for enlisted personnel utilized a spike base with a football shape pediment. The throat had two round vent holes on each side. It attached with domed screws. The spike was smooth. The chinscales were attached with a screw through rounded retainers known as "rosetten". The cockade was large one-piece construction with serrated edges. Visors were lined in leather.

Garde du Corps, Garde Kurassier, and Sixth kurassier helmet bodies were made of tombac with edge trim, front plate, and spike base in silver. The spike, chinscales, kleebatten, and posts were also of tombac. The enlisted pattern helmets were essentially made of the same material except they carried rosetten. Later, screws were added for the chinscales. Both the Garde du Corps and the Garde Kurassier wore a flying Prussian eagle as a spike replacement for Parade dress. The base of the eagle matched the shape of the spike base with officers being four sided and enlisted having a football form. Officer pattern eagles wore a golden crown with enlisted pattern having a silver crown.

All other Kurassier regiments were essentially the same helmet except for the sixth regiment. The officer and enlisted helmets of the remainder of the regiments were made of a polished steel body with edge trim, brads, front plate, chinscales, rosettes, posts, screws, and spike base in brass. The spike was polished steel.

There were a number of helmet style, size and form changes during it evolution. The hinged front visor used in the Model 1843 proved impractical and in 1853 it was moved to the inside of the body and fixed in position with pins. As with all Prussian units, in 1860 the "MIT GOTT FUR KOENIG" banner was added to the helmet front plate. The Model 1843/53 helmet proved too heavy for use in the field. Due to this in 1862 and again in 1867 a reduction in helmet size was done. Also in 1867, edge trim was added at the earpiece between the front and rear visors. Enlisted pattern helmets introduced screws instead of stylized posts for the chinscale attachment.

In 1889 the overall size and form of the enlisted pattern helmet was again changed. The two-stepped front visor was replaced by a rounded non-stepped visor. In addition, the overall size and weight of the helmet was reduced. In 1894 the issue helmets had model 1891 side posts and chinscales added. Due to the shortage of brass, in 1915 the Central Army command mandated that issue helmets were to have all metal trim made in a field gray finish and use chinstraps.

The Royal Saxon Garde Reiter, and Karabiner helmet regiments initially wore leather Raupenhelm (leather helmet with tall horse hair comb) helmet with until 1876. At that time, Saxony adopted essentially the same form as the Garde du Corps and Kurassier regiments. Garde Reiter and Garde Karabiner bodies were made of tombac with edge trim, front plate, and spike base in silver. The spike, chinscales, kleebatten, and posts were also of tombac. The enlisted pattern helmets were essentially the same material except they carried rosettes. Later, screws were added for the chinscales. Garde

Reiter and Karabiner issue helmets both had a distinctive ridge behind the spike base on all models, which was lacking on the Prussian helmets. In 1906, the Saxon Garde Reiter Regiment adopted a half raised Lion standing on the royal cipher as the spike replacement for parade dress. The Garde Karabinier wore a white plume to parade.

Jaeger zu Pferde

Jaeger zu Pferde regiments first came into being in 1905. Officers wore a bright nickeled steel body. The issue helmets for regiments 1 though 7 wore a blued steel body. The issue helmets for regiments 8 through 13 wore the leather helmet common to the Prussian line Dragoon regiments. The color of the trim varied with the regiment. In 1915 the enlisted helmets had the metal trim finished in a field gray and used chinstraps.

Dragoons

The Dragoon spiked helmet was introduced in 1842. In 1844 the 1st regiment was awarded the grand eagle of the grenadiers. They were awarded in 1854 the special grenadier style eagle with garde sword and eagle tipped scepter. In 1857, 1860, and 1867 the overall size of helmet was continually reduced. In 1871 the officer rosetten were made in one piece and issue helmets wore screw posts. The use of the Mod.1891 side lug used by enlisted troops of foot was adopted for use with the Dragoon helmet in 1894. Rounded style chinscales were designed to fit over the M91 post. The early style helmet had all officers and enlisted men plumes made of horsehair. In 1895 officers were to wear buffalo hair plumes and enlisted retained the use of horsehair plumes for parade. In 1897 the 3rd Dragoon regiment was awarded the flaming bomb rosetten and side posts. In 1899 the 9th Dragoon regiment was awarded the battle honor bandeau of "Peninsula-Waterloo" and the 16th regiment was awarded the battle honor bandeau of "Peninsula". In 1913 the 2nd Dragoon regiment was awarded a special device with the scepter of the grand elector of Brandenburg. The officer helmet device was a multiple piece with fine blue and red enamel. Issue helmets were in a silver finish. In 1915 the issue helmets metal parts were produced in field gray trim.

Some traits were common to all periods of this helmet. All the bodies were leather with squared front visors, except for the semi-rounded visor of the Hessen. All had cross spike bases and wore rounded scales. Most officers' helmets had a spike base with a pearl and ring trim and wore star retainers on the spike base. Issue helmets had the pearl without the ring and used domed retainers on the spike base. Fittings and trim were brass, tombac or matte silver. Exception to this rule was the Hessen helmets, which did not have the pearl or pearl with ring on these helmets. Also Hessen officers and issue helmets both wore domed retainer screws. Officers' trim and fittings were either gilt or silvered.

Uhlans

The first helmet adopted for use by the Prussian Uhlan was a small black leather skull-cap with a large boxy leather top. The sides of the top (the rabatte) were covered in a dark blue cloth. The flat top surface of the helmet (mortar board) was supported in back with a leather support. All helmets wore rounded chinscales.

The Uhlans of 1843 were changed in 1844. They were smaller and constructed of black lacquered leather. The rear leather support was no longer necessary. The rabatte colors were changed to match the unit epaulette colors. The Prussian eagle front plate was added to the front of the helmet at the top of the rabatte. The "Mit Gott Fur Koenig" was added to the eagle in 1860. In 1862 metal trim was added to the front visor.

A considerable change was seen in 1867 for issue helmets and in 1868 for officers. The helmet size was greatly reduced and the neck of the top was narrowed and tapered. The eagle was also moved to the front of the helmet body. The rabatte was made to be removable and was worn now only for parade.

In 1889 the neck size and mortarboard top sizes were reduced further. Vents were added to the neck of the top. In 1894 the issue helmets wore model 1891 side posts and appropriate chinscales. In 1915 the issue helmets were given removable metal tops, chinstraps and a field gray finish to the metal parts.

All of these helmets had leather bodies with a round front visor and the distinctive mortarboard top. All officers' helmets had trim and fittings in either gold or silver. Issue helmets had fittings and trim was brass, tombac, or matte silver.

During World War I these helmets were made of a variety of materials. Issue helmets were in field gray after 1915.

Hussars

The Hussar helmet of 1843 was a tall black and white colored felt body. In 1847 the helmet was given rounded chinscales and a brass unit number on the front of the body. A large black and white field badge was worn on the side of the helmet.

In 1860 the helmet size was reduced. The issue helmet was produced in brown seal fur. Officer's helmets were made of otter fur. This model had small fur covered front and rear visors. The field badge was moved to the top front of the helmet. The LeibGarde (Life Guard) units wore a star shaped front plate. The Leib hussar units wore a death head. In 1860 bandeaus with "Mit Gott Fur Koenig" were adopted for use. In 1861 the 7th Regiment was awarded the personal cipher for King Wilhelm of Prussia for use as a front plate. In 1888 the roman numeral "I" was added to distinguish between Kaiser Wilhelm I and the new Kaiser Wilhelm II. In 1894 the enlisted helmet adopted the use of 1891 chinscales.

Beginning May 5, 1912, officers were allowed to have helmets made of gray possum. Otter was still used until 1917.

Artillery

The construction and evolution of the artillery helmet essentially followed along the same lines as the infantry helmet. The artillery helmets differed very little from each other. The major difference was that field artillery wore rounded chinscales where the foot artillery wore flat chinscales.

These regiments used a symbolic ball top instead of the spike.

Train

Train units were developed for supplies and logistics. Originally, in 1842, train battalions used the spiked helmet. In 1863 train units adopted the use of the shako for the issue helmet while the officers retained the spiked helmet. The enlisted shako followed changes along the same lines as the Jaeger Battalions. The officer helmets followed the same changes along the same lines as the infantry helmet. The major difference is that train battalions wore rounded chinscales. In 1903 the issue helmet for the enlisted changed to the spiked helmet. Both train officers and enlisted wore black plumes to parade. In 1915 issue helmets were given field gray trim.

BAVARIA

Bavarian helmets evolved along a somewhat different line. The front plate saw several changes. From 1842-1848, they carried an "M" for Maximillian. From 1848 to 1864, the front plates carried an "L" for Ludwig. From 1864 – 1878, they carried the "M" for Maximillian III. In 1886 a new front plate was created utilizing the royal crest.

The Bavarian Kurassier helmets of 1842 had a crest or rauppe. This was a comb of fur, which ran across the spine of the helmet from front to back. The tall bodies were made of steel.

In 1878, the helmets changed to the more modern leather body with a cross spike base and spike. They were then incorporated into the Schwere Reiters (heavy cavalry) and Chevaleger (light cavalry) regiments.

The next change was in 1886 when the new front plate was adopted. The spike was fluted and the front visor corners were squared. The Schwere Reiter and Chevaleger wore a leather body raupenhelm (tall combed helmet), which evolved along the same lines as the kurassier.

The Bavarian Uhlans moved along a similar path as the Prussians. The old 1812 Tschapka was used until 1864. Then it was given the mortarboard type top and lions were added to the rosetten. In 1873 front visor trim was added. The Field badge was made oval instead of round. In 1886 the newly designed front plate was added. In 1891 the enlisted helmets were given the 1891 side posts. In 1915 they were given a removable metal top and carried chinstraps.

The Bavarian artillery units wore raupenhelm at first and then adopted the new style in 1886. The Bavarian Artillery Regiments did not initially adopt the use of the "ball" ornament as was done in Prussia. The foot artillery wore flat chinscales and the field artillery wore rounded chinscales. It was not until 1916 that all Bavarian Artillery Regiments wore a ball top instead of the spike. Bavarian train battalions wore the rounded chinscales and retained the fluted spike.

1

Garde du Corp, Garde Kurrasier, Garde Reiter, and Garde Karibinier

Preussen/Prussia

Officer	Garde du Corp / Garde Kurassier	Model 1843

Preussen/Prussia		
Enlisted Man	Garde du Corp / Garde Kurassier	Model 1867

	Preussen/Prussia	
Enlisted Man	Garde du Corp / Garde Kurassier	Model 1889

Preussen/Prussia

Enlisted Man | Garde du Corp / Garde Kurassier | Model 1889

To Parade

Preussen/Prussia

Enlisted Man Garde du Corps / Garde Kurassier Model 1894

Preussen/Prussia

Enlisted Man | Garde du Corps / Garde Kurassier | Model 1894

To Parade

Garde du Corps NCO

Preussen/Prussia

Officer — Garde du Corps / Garde Kurassier — Model 1899

To Parade

	Sachsen/Saxon	
Enlisted Man	Garde Reiter / Gardc Karabinier	Model 1894

One Year Volunteer	Sachsen/Saxon Garde Reiter To Parade	Model 1907

Reserve Officer	**Sachsen**/Saxon Garde Reiter To Parade	Model 1907

Reserve	**Sachsen**/Saxon	Model 1876
NCO	Garde Karabinier	
	To Parade	

Reserve Officer	Sachsen/Saxon Garde Karabinier	Model 1876

2

Kurassier

Bayern/Bavaria

Enlisted Man | Kurassier Rgmt. 1,2 | Model 1842

Bavaria/Bavaria

Enlisted Man	Kurassier Rgmt. 1,2	Model 1878

Enlisted Man	**Preussen**/Prussia Kurassier Rgmt. 1 After july 1, 1902	Model 1902

Enlisted Man	Preussen/Prussia Kurassier Rgmt. 1 After july 1, 1902	Model 1915

Preußen/Prussia

Officer Aspirrant | Kurassier Rgmt. 1 | Model 1902

After july 1, 1902

Officer	**Preussen**/Prussia Kurassier Rgmt. 1 After july 1, 1902	Model 1902

Preussen/Prussia		
Side View	Kurassier Rgmt. 1	Model 1902
Officer	After July 1, 1902	

	Preussen/Prussia	
Enlisted Man	Kurassier Rgmt. 2	Model 1867

Preussen/Prussia

Enlisted Man	Kurassier Rgmt. 2	Model 1894

Preussen/Prussia

Enlisted Man | Kurassier Rgmt. 2 | Model 1915

Preussen/Prussia

Officer | Kurassier Rgmt. 2 | Model 1899

Preussen/Prussia

Enlisted Man	Kurassier Rgmt. 3, 4, 5, 7, 8 Rgmt. 1 Before July 1, 1902	Model 1843

Enlisted Man	**Preussen**/Prussia Kurassier Rgmt. 3, 4, 5, 7, 8 Rgmt. 1 Before July 1, 1902	Model 1867

Preussen/Prussia

Enlisted Man — Kurassier Rgmt. 3,4,5,7,8 — Model 1894

Rgmt. 1 Before July 1, 1902

Preussen/Prussia

Officer	Kurassier Rgmt. 3,4,5,7,8 Rgmt. 1 Before July 1, 1902	Model 1899

Preussen/Prussia

Enlisted Man	Kurassier Rgmt. 6	Model 1867

Enlisted Man	**Preussen**/Prussia Kurassier Rgmt. 6	Model 1894

	Preussen/Prussia	
Officer	Kurassier Rgmt. 6	Model 1899

3

Jager zu Pferde

Preussen/Prussia

Enlisted Man	Jager zu Pferde Rgmt. 1-4, 7	Model 1905

Preussen/Prussia

Officer | Jager zu Pferde Rgmt. 1-4, 7 | Model 1905

Preussen/Prussia

Enlisted Man	Jager zu Pferde Rgmt. 8-13	Model 1913

Fahnrich	**Preussen**/Prussia Jager zu Pferde Rgmt. 1-4,7	Model 1915

Preussen/Prussia		
Fahnrich	Jager zu Pferde Rgmt. 8-13	Model 1913

	Preussen/Prussia	
Officer	Jager zu Pferde Rgmt. 8-13	Model 1915

4

Dragoons

	Baden/Baden	
Enlisted Man	Dragoon Rgmt. 20,21,22	Model 1894

	Baden/Baden	
Officer	Dragoon Rgmt. 20,21,22	Model 1899
	To Parade	

Baden/Baden		
Reserve Officer	Dragoon Rgmt. 20,21,22	Model 1899

Bayern/Bavaria

Officer	Chevauleger Rgmt. 1,3,5,7 Schwere Reiter Rgmt. 2	Model 1868

Enlisted Man	**Bayern**/Bavaria Chevauleger Rgmt. 1,3,5,7 Schwere Reiter Rgmt. 2	Model 1886

Bayern/Bavaria

Officer — Chevauleger Rgmt. 1,3,5,7 — Model 1886

Schwere Reiter Rgmt. 2

	Bayern/Bavaria	
Enlisted Man	Chevauleger Rgmt. 2,4,6,8 Schwere Reiter Rgmt. 1	Model 1886

Bayern/Bavaria

One Year Volunteer	Chevauleger Rgmt. 2,4,6,8 Schwere Reiter Rgmt. 1	Model 1886

	Bayern/Bavaria	
Officer	Chevauleger Rgmt. 2, 4, 6, 8	Model 1886
	Schwere Reiter Rgmt. 1	
	To Parade	

Prussian royal family in Cavalry uniforms.

Hessen/Hessen

Enlisted Man — Dragoon Rgmt 23, 24 — Model 1894

Hessen/Hessen

Officer | Dragoon Rgmt 23, 24 | Model 1872

To Parade

Hessen/Hessen		
Officer	Dragoon Rgmt 23, 24	Model 1872

Hessen/Hessen

Officer	Dragoon Rgmt 23/After April 6, 1915 To Parade	Model 1915

Mecklenburg-Schwerin/

Enlisted Man	Mecklenburg-Schwerin Dragoon Rgmt 17	Model 1848

Officer	**Mecklenburg-Schwerin/** Mecklenburg-Schwerin Dragoon Rgmt 17 To Parade	Model 1895

Enlisted Man	**Mecklenburg-Schwerin/** Mecklenburg-Schwerin Dragoon Rgmt 18	Model 1895

Reserve Officer	**Mecklenburg-Schwerin/** Mecklenburg-Schwerin Dragoon Rgmt 18	Model 1895

Oldenburg/Oldenburg

Enlisted Man | Dragoon Rgmt 19 | Model 1894

	Oldenburg/Oldenburg	
Officer	Dragoon Rgmt 19	Model 1899

Preussen/Prussia

Enlisted Man | Garde Dragoon Rgmt. 1 | Model 1860

Preussen/Prussia

Enlisted Man	Garde Dragoon Rgmt. 1	Model 1871

Preussen/Prussia

Enlisted Man — Garde Dragoon Rgmt. 1 — Model 1894

To Parade

Officer	**Preussen**/Prussia Garde Dragoon Rgmt. 1 To Parade	Model 1899

Preussen/Prussia

Landwehr Officer | Garde Dragoon Rgmt. 1 | Model 1899

Preussen/Prussia

Officer | Garde Dragoon Rgmt. 2 | Model 1899

Preussen/Prussia

Enlisted Man	Dragoon Rgmt. 1	Model 1894

	Preussen/Prussia	
Officer	Dragoon Rgmt. 1	Model 1899

Preussen/Prussia

Reserver Officer | Dragoon Rgmt. 1 | Model 1899

	Preussen/Prussia	
Enlisted Man	Dragoon Rgmt. 2	Model 1913

Preussen/Prussia

Fahnrich | Dragoon Rgmt. 2 | Model 1913

To Parade

Preussen/Prussia

Officer | Dragoon Rgmt. 2 | Model 1913

Preussen/Prussia

Officer	Dragoon Rgmt. 2 To Parade	Model 1913

Preussen/Prussia

Landwehr Officer	Dragoon Rgmt. 2	Model 1915

Preussen/Prussia

Officer Wappen | Dragoon Rgmt. 2 | Model 1913

Preussen/Prussia

Enlisted Man | Dragoon Rgmt. 3 | Model 1894

Preussen/Prussia		
Officer	Dragoon Rgmt. 3	Model 1899

Preussen/Prussia

Landwehr Officer | Dragoon Rgmt. 3 | Model 1899

Preussen/Prussia

Enlisted Man	Dragoon Rgmt. 4, 5, 6, 10, 12, 15	Model 1894

Preussen/Prussia		
Officer	Dragoon Rgmt. 4, 5, 6, 10, 12, 15	Model 1899

Preussen/Prussia		
Enlisted Man	Dragoon Rgmt. 7, 8, 9, 11, 13, 14	Model 1894

Preussen/Prussia

Landwehr Officer | Dragoon Rgmt. 7, 8, 9, 11, 13, 14 | Model 1860

Preussen/Prussia

Landwehr Officer Dragoon Rgmt. 7, 8, 9, 11, 13, 14 Model 1899

Enlisted Man	Preussen/Prussia Dragoon Rgmt. 9 To Parade	Model 1899

Preussen/Prussia

Officer	Dragoon Rgmt. 9	Model 1899

Landwehr Officer	**Preussen**/Prussia Dragoon Rgmt. 9 To Parade	Model 1899

	Preussen/Prussia	
Enlisted Man	Dragoon Rgmt. 16	Model 1899

Preussen/Prussia

Officer | Dragoon Rgmt. 16 | Model 1899

To Parade

Preussen/Prussia

Landwehr Officer	Dragoon Rgmt. 16 To Parade	Model 1899

Württemburg/Wurttemburg

Officer | Dragoon Rgmt. 25 | Model 1871

Wurttemburg/Wurttemburg

Enlisted Man	Dragoon Rgmt. 26	Model 1905

Wurttemburg/Wurttemburg		
Officer	Dragoon Rgmt. 26	Model 1905

5

Hussars

Braunschweig/Brunswick

Fahnrich | Hussar Rgmt. 17 | Model 1894

To Parade

Officer	**Braunschweig**/Brunswick Hussar Rgmt. 17 To Parade	Model 1871

Preussen/Prussia

Enlisted Man | Leib Garde Hussar Rgmt. 1 | Model 1894

Preussen/Prussia

Fahnrich | Leib Garde Hussar | Model 1894

To Parade

Officer	Preussen/Prussia Leib Garde Hussar To Parade	Model 1871

Officer	**Preussen**/Prussia Leib Hussar Rgmt. 1 To Parade	Model 1871

Preussen/Prussia

Officer | Leib Hussar Rgmt. 2 | Model 1871

To Parade

Preussen/Prussia

Officer — Hussar Rgmt. 3 — Model 1871

To Parade

Preussen/Prussia

Reserve Officer | Hussar Rgmt. 4 | Model 1871

To Parade

NCO	**Preussen**/Prussia Hussar Rgmt. 5 To Parade	Model 1871

Preussen/Prussia

Reserve Officer

Hussar Rgmt. 5
To Parade

Model 1871

Reserve Officer	**Preussen**/Prussia Hussar Rgmt. 6 To Parade	Model 1871

Preussen/Prussia

Officer — Hussar Rgmt. 7 — Model 1871

To Parade

Preussen/Prussia

Reserve Officer | Hussar Rgmt. 7 | Model 1871

To Parade

Preussen/Prussia

Officer

Hussar Rgmt. 8

To Parade

Model 1871

Preussen/Prussia

Officer

Hussar Rgmt. 9

To Parade

Model 1871

Preussen/Prussia

NCO	Hussar Rgmt. 10 To Parade	Model 1871

Preussen/Prussia

Officer	Hussar Rgmt. 10 To Parade	Model 1871

Preussen/Prussia

Officer

Hussar Rgmt. 11 and 13

To Parade

Model 1871

Reserve Officer	**Preussen**/Prussia Hussar Rgmt. 12 To Parade	Model 1871

Preussen/Prussia

Officer | Hussar Rgmt. 12/After January 24, 1899 | Model 1871

To Parade

Preussen/Prussia

Officer — Hussar Rgmt. 16 — Model 1871

To Parade

Officer	Sachsen/Saxon Hussar Rgmt. 18 To Parade	Model 1871

Officer	**Sachsen**/Saxon Hussar Rgmt. 19 To Parade	Model 1871

Sachsen/Saxon		
Enlisted Man	Uhlan Rgmt. 20	Model 1895

Sachsen/Saxon		
Officer	Hussar Rgmt. 20 To Parade	Model 1871

6

Uhlans

Bayern/Bavaria

NCO | Uhlan Rgmt. 1 | Model 1886

Officer	**Bayern**/Bavaria Uhlan Rgmt. 1 To Parade	Model 1886

	Bayern/Bavaria	
Reserve Officer	Uhlan Rgmt. 2	Model 1886
	To Parade	

Preussen/Prussia

Officer | Garde Uhlan Rgmt. 1 | Model 1899

To Parade

Preussen/Prussia		
Officer	Garde Uhlan Rgmt. 3	Model 1899
	To Parade	

Preussen/Prussia

Officer	Uhlan Rgmt. 1	Model 1899
	To Parade	

Preussen/Prussia

Officer	Uhlan Rgmt. 2 To Parade	Model 1899

Preussen/Prussia

Officer | Uhlan Rgmt. 3 | Model 1899

To Parade

Officer	**Preussen**/Prussia Uhlan Rgmt. 5 To Parade	Model 1899

Preussen/Prussia

Officer | Uhlan Rgmt. 7 After January 16, 1913 | Model 1913

To Parade

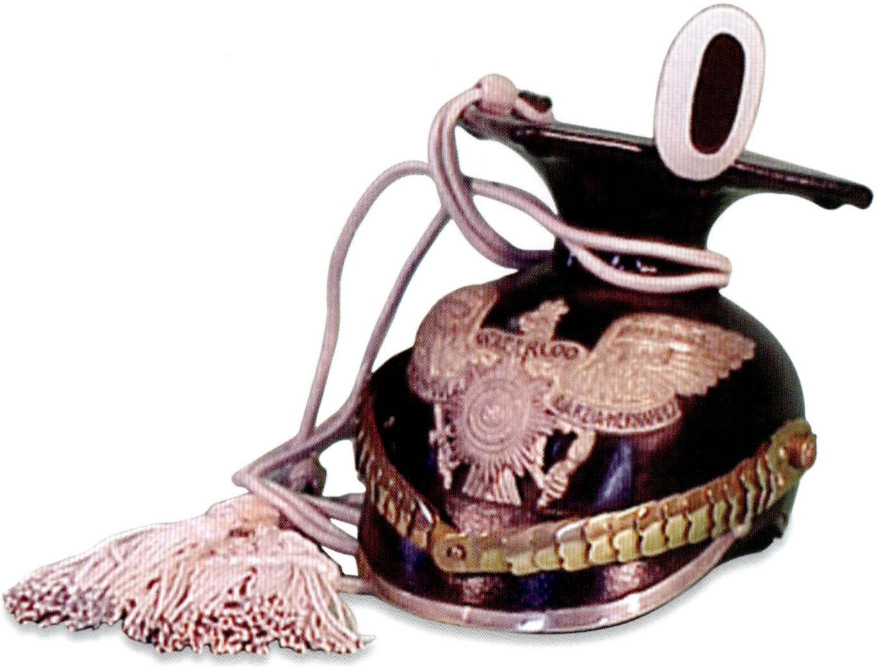

Preussen/Prussia

Enlisted Man — Uhlan Rgmt. 13 After January 24, 1899 — Model 1899

Preussen/Prussia

Officer | Uhlan Rgmt. 13 After January 24, 1899 To Parade | Model 1899

Preussen/Prussia

Officer	Uhlan Rgmt. 14 After January 24, 1899 To Parade	Model 1899

	Sachsen/Saxon	
Officer	Uhlan Rgmt. 17	Model 1899
	To Parade	

Sachsen/Saxon

Officer | Uhlan Rgmt. 18 | Model 1899

To Parade

Enlisted Man	Sachsen/Saxon Uhlan Rgmt. 21 To Parade	Model 1894

Sachsen/Saxon

Officer	Uhlan Rgmt. 21 To Parade	Model 1899

Wurttemburg/Wurttemburg

Officer | Uhlan Rgmt. 19 | Model 1889

To Parade

Württemburg/Wurttemburg

Officer	Uhlan Rgmt. 20 To Parade	Model 1889

7

Artillery

	Preussen/Prussia	
Officer	General of Artillery	Model 1889

Wurttemburg/Wurttemburg

Officer	General of Aritllery	Model 1889

Baden/Baden

Enlisted Man | Field Artillery Rgmt. 14, 30, 50, 66, 76 | Model 1894

Baden/Baden

Officer	Field Artillery Rgmt. 14, 30, 50, 66, 76	Model 1899

	Baden/Baden	
Landwehr Officer	Field Artillery Rgmt. 14, 30, 50, 66, 76	Model 1899

Bayern/Bavaria

Enlisted Man | Field Artillery Rgmt. 1-12 | Model 1886

Bayern/Bavaria		
Officer	Field Artillery Rgmt. 1-12	Model 1886

Bayern/Bavaria

Enlisted Man	Field Artillery Rgmt. 1-12	Model 1916

Bayern/Bavaria

Officer	Field Artillery Rgmt. 1-12	Model 1916

Bayern/Bavaria

Reserve Officer — Field Artillery Rgmt. 1-12 — Model 1916

	Hessen/Hessen	
Officer	Field Artillery Rgmt. 25, 64	Model 1895

Hessen/Hessen

Landwehr Officer — Field Artillery Rgmt. 25, 64 — Model 1895

Officer	Hessen/Hessen Field Artillery Rgmt. 25 After April 16, 1915	Model 1915

14

Mecklenburg-Schwerin		
Enlisted Man	Mecklenburg-Schwerin Field Artillery Rgmt. 60	Model 1915

Mecklenburg-Schwerin

Officer

Mecklenburg-Schwerin
Field Artillery Rgmt. 60

Model 1899

Enlisted Man	**Mecklenburg-Strelitz** Mecklenburg-Strelitz Field Artillery Rgmt. 24/3 Batt.	Model 1895

Mecklenburg-Strelitz

Officer | Mecklenburg-Strelitz | Model 1899

Field Artillery Rgmt. 24/3 Batt.

Oldenburg / Oldenburg

Enlisted Man — Field Artillery Rgmt. 62/2 and 3 Batt. — Model 1915

Oldenburg / Oldenburg

Officer — Field Artillery Rgmt. 62/2 and 3 Batt. — Model 1899

Preussen/Prussia

Enlisted Man | Garde Field Artillery Rgmt. 1, 2, 3, 4 | Model 1895

Preussen/Prussia

Officer — Garde Field Artillery Rgmt. 1, 2, 3, 4 — Model 1899

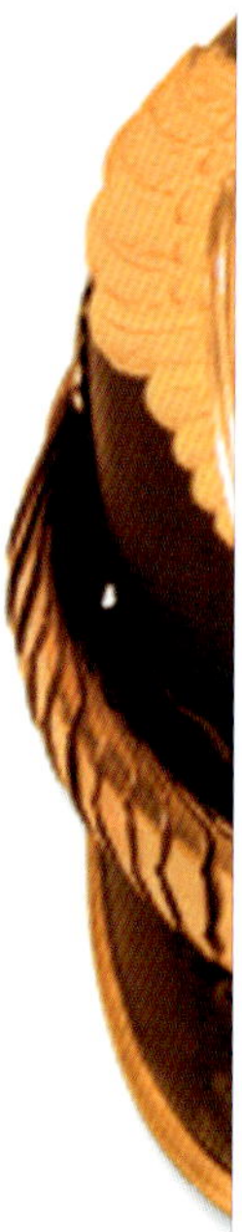

Landwehr (

Preussen/Prussia

Enlisted Man — Field Artillery Rgmt. 1, 2 — Model 1895

Preussen/Prussia

Officer | Field Artillery Rgmt. 1, 2 | Model 1899

Preussen/Prussia

Officer	Field Artillery Rgmt. 2/3rd Company and Rgmt. 3/6th Company	Model 1899

Preussen/Prussia

Enlisted Man	Field Artillery Rgmt. 4-5, 7-9, 11, 15-44, 26, 27, 31, 33-45, 46/II-III, 47, 51-59, 62-63, 67, 69-75	Model 1895

Preussen/Prussia

One Year Volunteer	Field Artillery Rgmt. 4-5, 7-9, 11, 15-44, 26, 27, 31, 33-45, 46/II-III, 47, 51-59, 62-63, 67, 69-75	Model 1899

Enlisted Man	**Preussen**/Prussia Field Artillery Rgmt. 10	Model 1895

Preussen/Prussia

Officer	Field Artillery Rgmt. 10	Model 1899

Preussen/Prussia

Reserve Officer	Field Artillery Rgmt. 10	Model 1899

Preussen/Prussia

Enlisted Man	Field Artillery Rgmt. 10/2 After Jan. 24, 1909 46/2 After Oct. 1, 1909, 35/2 After Oct. 1, 1913	Model 1895

Preussen/Prussia

Enlisted	Field Artillery Rgmt. 26/2, 35/1, 2, 4, 46/2 Batt.	Model 1899

Preussen/Prussia

Officer Field Artillery Rgmt. 26/2, 35/1, 2, 4, 46/2 Batt. Model 1899

Sachsen/Saxon		
Enlisted Man	Field Artillery Rgmt. 12, 28, 32, 48, 64, 68, 77, 78	Model 1895

Sachsen/Saxon

Officer	Field Artillery Rgmt. 12, 28, 32, 48, 64, 68, 77, 78	Model 1899

	Wurttemburg/Wurttemburg	
Enlisted Man	Field Artillery Rgmt. 13, 29, 49, 65	Model 1895

Wurttemburg/Wurttemburg

Officer | Field Artillery Rgmt. 13, 29, 49, 65 | Model 1899

Baden/Baden

Enlisted Man | Foot Artillery Rgmt. 14 | Model 1895

Baden/Baden

Officer — Foot Artillery Rgmt. 14 — Model 1899

	Bayern/Bavaria	
Enlisted Man	Foot Artillery Rgmt. 1, 2, 3	Model 1886

Officer	**Bayern**/Bavaria Foot Artillery Rgmt. 1, 2, 3 To Parade	Model 1886

	Bayern/Bavaria	
Enlisted Man	Foot Artillery Rgmt. 1, 2, 3	Model 1916

Reserve Officer	**Bayern**/Bavaria Foot Artillery Rgmt. 1, 2, 3	Model 1916

Preussen/Prussia

Enlisted Man | Garde Foot Artillery | Model 1895

Preussen/Prussia

Officer — Garde Foot Artillery — Model 1899

Preussen/Prussia

Officer — Garde Foot Artillery 4th Company — Model 1899

Preussen/Prussia

Enlisted Man — Foot Artillery Rgmt. 1, 2, 3, 6 — Model 1895

Preussen/Prussia

Officer	Foot Artillery Rgmt. 1, 2, 3, 6	Model 1899

	Preussen/Prussia	
Enlisted Man	Foot Artillery Rgmt. 4, 5, 7-11, 13, 15, 18	Model 1895

Preussen/Prussia

Officer — Foot Artillery Rgmt. 4, 5, 7-11, 13, 15, 18 — Model 1899

Preussen/Prussia		
Landwehr Officer	Foot Artillery Rgmt. 4, 5, 7-11, 13, 15, 18	Model 1899

Schießübung
1908.
Münsingen.

Preussen/Prussia

Enlisted Man — Foot Artillery Rgmt. 2/3 Company — Model 1895

Sachsen/Saxon

Enlisted Man | Foot Artillery Rgmt. 12 | Model 1895

Sachsen/Saxon

Officer Foot Artillery Rgmt. 12 Model 1899

8

Train

Baden/Baden

Enlisted Man	Train Battalion 14	Model 1894

Baden/Baden

Officer

Train Battalion 14

To Parade

Model 1899

Bayern/Bavaria

Enlisted Man	Train Battalion 1, 2, 3	Model 1886

2nd Rhenish Hussar Regt. **No.9**	1815	Strassburg
Magdeburg Hussar Regt. No. **10**	1813	Stendal
2nd Westfallen Hussar R. No. **11**	1813	Krefeld
Thuringian Hussar Regt. No. **12**	1791	Torgau
Hussar R. King Umberto of Italy (1st Electoral Hessen) No. **13**	1813	Diedenhofen
Hussar Regt. Landgrave Friedrich II of Hesse-Homburg (2nd Electoral Hessen) No. **14**	1813	Kassel
Hussar Reg. Queen Wilhelmina of the Netherlands (Hannover) No. **15**	1803	Wandsbek
Hussar Regt. Kaiser Franz Joseph of Austria (Schleswig-Holstein) No. **16**	1866	Schleswig
Braunschweig Hus. Regt. No. **17**	1809	Braunschweig
Royal Saxon Hussar Regt. King Albert No. **18**	1734	Gossenhain
Royal Saxon 2nd Hussar Regt. No **19**	1791	Grimma
Royal Saxon 3rd Hussar Regt. No. **20**	1910	Bautzen

Jaeger zu Pferde - Mounted Rifle

Jaeger zu Pferde No. 1	1905	Posen
Jaeger zu Pferde No. 2	1905	Langensalza
Jaeger zu Pferde No. **3**	1905	Colmar
Jaeger zu Pferde No. 4	1906	Graudenz
Jaeger zu Pferde No. **5**	1908	Muhlhausen
Jaeger zu Pferde No. **6**	1910	Erfurt
Jaeger zu Pferde No. 7	1913	Trier
Jaeger zu Pferde No. 8	1913	Trier
Jaeger zu Pferde No. 9	1913	Insterburg
Jaeger zu Pferde No.10	1913	Angerburg
Jaeger zu Pferde No. 11	1913	Tarnowitz
Jaeger zu Pferde No. 12	1913	Avold
Jaeger zu Pferde No. 13	1913	Saarlouis

Royal Bavarian Cavalry

1st Heavy Cavalry Regt.	1814	Munich
Prince Karl of Bavaria		
2nd Heavy Cavalry Regt.	1815	Landshut
1st Light Cavalry Regt.	1682	Nuremberg
Tsar Nicholas of Russia		
2nd Light Cavalry Regt.	1682	Regensburg
		Taxis
3rd Light Cavalry Regt.	1724	Dieuze
4th Light Cavalry Regt.	1744	Augsburg
5th Light Cavalry Regt.	1776	Saargemund
Archduke Friedrich of Austria		
6th Light Cavalry Regt.	1803	Bayreuth
Prince Albrecht of Prussia		
7th Light Cavalry Regt.	1905	Straubing
Prince Alfons		
8th Light Cavalry Regt.	1909	Dillingen
1st Uhlan Regt.	1863	Bamberg
Kaiser Wilhelm II –King of Prussia		
King's **2nd** Uhlan Regt.	1863	Ansbach

Field Artillery

1ST Guard Field Art. Regt.	1816	Berlin
2nd Guard Field Art. Regt.	1872	Potsdam
3rd Guard Field Art. Regt.	1899	Berlin
4th Guard Field Art. Regt	1899	Potsdam
F. Art. R. Prince August	1772	Gumbinnen
of Prussia (1st Lithuanian) No.**1**		Insterburg
1st Pommeranian Fld Art. Regt. No **2**	1808	Kolberg
		Belgard
Fld. Art. Regt. General	1816	Brandenburg
Ordnance (1st Brandenburg) No**. 3**		
Fld. Art. Regt. Prince Luit-	1816	Magdeburg
pold of Bavaria (Magdeburg) No**. 4**		
Fld. Art. R. v. Podbielski	1816	Sprottau
(1st Lower Silesian) No**. 5**		
Fld. Art. Regt. v. Puecker	1808	Breslau
(1st Silesian) No. **6**		

1st Westfallen Fld. Art. Regt. No. 7	1816	Wesel
Fld .A. R. v. Holtzendorff (1st Rhenish) No**. 8**	1816	Saarbrucken
Fld. Art. R. Field Marshall Graf Waldersee (Schleswig) No. 9	1866	Itzehoe
Fld. Art. R. v. Scharnhorst (1st Hannover) No. **10**	1803	Hannover
1st Electoral Hessen Fld. Art. Regt. (1st Saxon) No. **12**	1813	Casel
Fld. Art. R. King Karl (1st Wurttemberg) No. **13**	1736	Ulm
Fld. Ar. Regt. Grand Duke (1st Baden) No. **14**	1850	Karlsruhe
1st Upper Alsatian Fld. Art. Regt. No. **15**	1871	Saarburg
1st Eas Prussian Fld. Art. Regt. No. **16**	1872	Koenigsberg
2nd Pommeranian Fld. Art. Regt. No. **17**	1872	Bromberg
F.A.R. Ordnance General (2nd Brandenburg) No. **18**	1872	Frankfurt/O
1st Thuringian Field Art. Regt. No. **19**	1872	Erfurt
1st Posen F. A. R. No **20**	1872	Posen
Fld Art. R. v. Clausewitz (1st Upper Silesian) No. **21**	1872	Neisse
2nd Westfallen Field Art. Regt. No. **22**	1872	Munster
2nd Rhenish F.A.R. No. **23**	1872	Koblenz
Holstein Fld. A. R. No**. 24**	1872	Gustrow
Grand Ducal Art. Corps (1st Grand Ducal Hessen) Field Art. Regt. No**. 25**	1790	Darmstadt
2nd Hannover Field Art. Regt. No. **26**	1872	Verden
1st Nassau F.A.R. No **27**	1833	Mainz
Royal Saxon 2nd Field Art. Regt. No. **28**	1872	Bautzen

2nd Wurttemberg Field Art. Regt. –Prince Luitpold of Bavaria No. **29**	1736	Ludwigsburg
2nd Baden F.A.R. No**. 30**	1872	Rastatt
1st Lower Alsatian Field Art. Regt. No. **31**	1881	Hagenau
Royal Saxon 3rd Field Art. Regt. No **32**	1889	Riesa
1st Lorraine F.A.R. No. **33**	1890	Metz
2nd Lorraine F.A.R. No. **34**	1890	Metz
1st West Prussian Fld. Art. Regt. No **35**	1890	Deutsch-Eylau
2nd West Prussian Fld. Art. Regt. No. **36**	1890	Danzig
2nd Lithuanian Fld. Art. Regt. No**. 37**	1899	Insterburg
Near Pommeranian Fld. Art. Regt. No. **38**	1899	Stettin
Kurmark F.A.R. No. **39**	1899	Perlebeg
Altmark F.A.R. No. **40**	1899	Burg
2nd Lower Silesian Field Art. Regt. No**. 41**	1899	Glogau
2nd Silesian F.A.R. No **42**	1899	Schweidnitz
Cleves F.A.R. No. **43**	1899	Wesel
Trier Fld. A. R. No. **44**	1899	Trier
Lauenburg F.A.R. No. **45**	1899	Altona
Lower Saxon Fld. Art. Regt. No. **46**	1899	Wolfebuttel
2nd Electoral Hessen Fld. Art. Regt. No. **47**	1899	Fulda
Royal Saxon Fld. Art. Regt. No. **48**	1899	Dresden
3rd Wurttemberg Fld. Art. Regt. No. **49**	1899	Ulm
3rd Baden F.A.R. No **50**	1899	Karlsruhe
2nd Upper Alsatian Fld. Art. Regt. **51**	1899	Strassburg
2nd East Prussian Fld. Art. Regt. No. **52**	1899	Koenigsberg

Far Pommeranian Fld. Art. Regt. No**. 53**	1899	Bromberg
Neumark F.A.R. No **54**	1899	Custrin
2nd Thuringian Fld. Art. Regt. No. **55**	1899	Naumberg
2nd Posen F.A.R. No **56**	1899	Lissa
2nd Upper Silesian Fld. Art. Regt. No. **57**	1899	Neustadt
Minden F. A. R. No. **58**	1899	Minden
Berg Fld. A. R. No. **59**	1899	Cologne
Grand Ducal Mecklenburg Fld. Art. Regt. No. **60**	1899	Schwerin
2nd Grand Ducal Hessen Fld. Art. Regt. No. **61**	1899	Darmstadt
East Frisian Fld. Art. Regt. No**. 62**	1899	Oldenburg
2nd Nassau F.A.R. No. **63**	1899	Frankfurt/m
Royal Saxon 5th Fld. Art. Regt. No**. 64**	1899	Pirna
4th Wurttemberg Fld. Art. Regt. No. **65**	1899	Ludwigsburg
4th Baden F.A.R. No. **66**	1899	Lahr
2nd Lower Alsatian Fld. Art. Regt. No. **67**	1899	Hagenau
Royal Saxon 6th Fld. Art. Regt. No. **68**	1899	Riesa
3rd Lorraine F.A.R. No. **69**	1899	St. Avold
4th Lorraine F.A.R. No**. 70**	1899	Metz
Field Art. Regt . No**. 71** Gross-Komtur	1899	Graudenz
Field Art.Regt. No**. 72** Hochmeister	1899	Marienwerder
1st Masurian Fld Art. Regt. No. **73**	1899	Allenstein
Torgau F.A.R. No **74**	1899	Torgau
Mansfeld F.A.R. No **75**	1899	Halle
5th Baden F.A.R. No**. 76**	1899	Freiberg
Royal Saxon 7h Fld. Art. Regt. No. **77**	1899	Leipzig
Royal Saxon 8th Fld. Art. Regt. No. **78**	1901	Wurzen
3rd East Prussian Fld. Art. Regt. No. **79**	1912	Osterode

3rd Upper Alsatian Fld. Art. Regt. No. **80**	1912	Colmar
Thorn F.A.R. No. **81**	1912	Thorn
2nd Masurian Fld. Art. Regt. No. **82**	1912	Rastenburg
3rd Rhenish Fld. Art. Regt. No. **83**	1912	Bonn
Strassburg F.A.R. No. **84**	1912	Strassburg
Field Gunnery School	1867	Juterbog

Foot Artillery

Guard Foot Art. Regt.	1865	Spandau
Foot Art. Regt. v. Linger (East Prussian) No.**1**	1864	Koenigsberg
Foot Art. R. v. Hindersin (1st Pommeranian) No.**2**	1865	Swinemunde
Ft. Art. Regt. Ordnance General (Brandenburg) No. **3**	1864	Mainz
Foot Art. Regt. Encke (Magdeburg) No. **4**	1864	Magdeburg
Lower Silesian Foot Art. Regt. No. **5**	1865	Posen
Foot Art. R. v. Dieskau (Silesian) No. **6**	1865	Neisse
Westfallen Foot Art. Regt. No. **7**	1864	Cologne
Rhenish Ft. Art. R. No. **8**	1864	Metz
Scheswig-Holstein Foot Regt. No. **9**	1893	Ehrnbreitstein
Lower Saxon Foot Art. Regt. No. **10**	1871	Strassburg
1st West Prussian Foot Art. Regt. No. **11**	1881	Thorn
1st Royal Saxon Foot Art. Regt. No. **12**	1873	Metz
Hohenzollern Foot Art. Regt. No. **13**	1805	Ulm
Baden Ft. Art R. No **14**	1893	Strassburg
2nd Pommeranian Foot Art. Regt. No. **15**	1893	Bromberg
Lorraine Foot Art. Regt. No. **16**	1912	Metz
2nd West Prussian Foot Art. Regt. No. **17**	1911	Pillau
Thuringian Foot Art. Regt. No. **18**	1912	Niederzwehren
2nd Royal Saxon Foot Art. Regt. No. **19**	1912	Dresden
Lauenburg Foot Art. Regt. No. **20**	1912	Altona
Foot Art. Gunnery School	1867	Juterbog

Bavarian Army Artillery Regiments

Field Artillery

1st Field Artillery Regt. Prince Regent Luitpold	1824	Munich.
2nd Field Art. Regt. Horn	1824	Wurzburg
3rd F A. R. Prince Leopold	1848	Grafenwohr
4th Field Art. Regt. King	1859	Augsburg
5th Field Art. Regt. King Alonso XIII of Spain	1890	Landau
6th Field Art. Regt. Prince Ferdinand of Bourbon, Duke of Calabria	1900	Furth
7th Field Art. Regt. Prince Regent Luitpold	1900	Munich
8th Field Art. Regt. Prince Heinrich of Prussia	1901	Nuremberg
9th Field Art. Regt.	1901	Lundberg
10th Field Art. Regt.	1901	Erlangen
11th Field Art. Regt.	1901	Wurzburg
12th Field Art. Regt.	1901	Landau/Pfalz

Foot Artillery (continued)

1st Foot Artillery Regt.	1873	Munich
2nd Foot Artillery Regt.	1873	Metz
3rd Foot artillery Regt.	1912	Ingolstadt

Train Battalions

Guard Train Battalion	1853	Berlin
East Prussian Train Bat. No.**1**	1856	Koenigsberg
Pommeranian Train Bat. No**. 2**	1853	Alt-Damm
Brandenburg Train Bat. No. **3**	1853	Spandau
Magdeburg Train Bat. No. **4**	1853	Magdeburg
Lower Silesian Train Bat**. 5**	1853	Posen
Silesian Train Bat. No. **6**	1853	Breslau
Westfallen Train Bat. No **7**	1853	Munster
1st Rhenish Train No**. 8**	Bat.	1853 Koblenz

Schleswig-Holstein Train Bat**. 9**	1866	Rendsberg
Hannover Train Bat. No. **10**	1866	Hannover
Electoral Hessen Train Bat. No. **11**	1854	Kassel
Royal Saxon Train Bat. No. **12**	1849	Dresden
Wurttemberg Train Bat. No. **13**	1871	Ludwigsburg
Baden Train Bat. No. **14**	1864	Durlach
Alsatian Train Bat. No. **15**	1871	Strassburg
Lorraine Train Bat. No. **16**	1890	Saarlouis
West Prussian Train Bat. No.**17**	1890	Danzig**1**ST
Grand Ducal Hessen Train Bat. No. **18**	1890	Darmstadt
Royal Saxon Train Bat. No**. 19**	1899	Leipzig
Masurian Train Bat. No. **20**	1912	Mareinberg
2nd Rhenih Train Bat. No**. 21**	1912	Forbach

Bavarian Train Battalions

1st Train Battalion	1872	Munich
2nd Train Battalion	1872	Wurzburg
3rd Train Battalion	1900	Furth

Bibliography

Museums

Bayerische Armee Museum, Ingolstadt, Germany
Fort de la Pompelle, Reims, France
Kavallerie Museum Vornholz, Schloss, Ostenfelde im Westfallen, Germany
Wehrgeschichtliches Museum, Schloss, Rastatt, Germany

Sources

Henckel, Carl. *ATLAS DES DEUTSCHEN REICHSHEERES*, 1902, reprint J.H. Bielitz & W. Eger, Wallertheim, 1984.

Hermann, Rainer: *MILITAERISCHE KOPFBEDECKUNGEN der KAISERZEIT*, Motorbuch Verlag, Stuttgart, 1999.

Kraus, Juergen, *DIE FELDGRAUE UNIFORMIERGUNG des DEUTSCHEN HEEREN 1907-1918 Bande I- II*, Motorbuch Verlag, Stuttgart, 2000.

Kube, Jan, *MILITARIA-HELMETS and UNIFORMS 1729-1918*, Schiffer Military History, West Chester, 1990.

Laine, Didier, *L'ARMEE ALLEMANDE en 1914*, Chromos Service, Paris, 1984
Laine, Didier, *LA REPERTOIRE de L'ARMEE ALLEMANDE 1914*, Diffusions Histoire, Chennevieres, 1998.

Larcarde, Jean-Louis, *CASQUES' a POINTE 1842-1918 – TROUPES a PIED*, Jacques Granchier, Paris, 1983.

Mueller, Heinrich, *EUROPAEISCHE HELME*, Verlag der DDR, Berlin 1971.

Pietsche, Paul, *DIE FORMATIONS und UNIFORMIERUNGS GESCHICHTE des PREUSSISCHEN HEERES 1908-1914 Bande I-II*, Verlag Gerhard Schulz, Hamburg 1966.

Notes

Notes

Notes

Notes

Notes